THE LION

THE BIG CAT DISCOVERY LIBRARY

Lynn M. Stone

Rourke Enterprises, Inc.
Vero Beach, Florida 32964

PHOTO CREDITS
© Lynn M. Stone: Pages 1, 4, 7, 8, 10, 12-13, 15, 17, 21 and
cover; © James P. Rowan: Page 18

ACKNOWLEDGEMENTS

The author wishes to thank the following for photographic
assistance in the preparation of this book: Miami Metrozoo;
Chester Zoo, Chester, U.K.

Library of Congress Cataloging-in-Publication Date
Stone, Lynn M.
    Lions / Lynn M. Stone.
    p. cm. — (The big cat discovery library)
    Includes index.
    Summary: An introduction to the physical characteristics,
habits, natural habitat, relationship to humans, and
future of the lion, often called "The King of Beasts".
    ISBN 0-86592-501-1
    1. Lions—Juvenile literature [1. Lions.] I. Title.
II. Series: Stone, Lynn M. Big cat discovery library.
QL737.C23S77 1989   89-32641
599.74'428—dc20   CIP
                                    AC

TABLE OF CONTENTS

THE LION

The lion *(Panthera leo)* is often called "The King of Beasts" or "The King of the Jungle". The lion isn't really a king. Like the kings of olden times, though, the lion is very powerful. Where lions prowl, other animals give way.

The lion is one of the biggest cats. In fact, the lion is second in size among the cats. Only tigers are larger.

Along with its great size, the lion has a mighty voice. The lion's roar has reminded people of thunder. Some African tribesmen say the lion's roar is saying, "I am lord of this land". There is some truth to that.

African Lioness

THE LION'S COUSINS

The lion is related to all cats, or **felines**—tigers, jaguars, leopards, and others. Like them, the lion is a **carnivore**, or meat-eater. Also like the other cats, the lion has short jaws, a very flexible body, sharp claws, and sharp teeth.

The lion's closest cousins are big cats that can roar—the tiger, leopard, and jaguar. Among these cats, the tiger is most like the lion. Captive lions and tigers have mated and produced "tiglons" and "ligers."

There is just one kind, or **species**, of lion. However, some differences between groups of lions do exist. The Indian lion, for example, does not have a thick mane like some African lions.

Indian (Asian) Lioness

HOW THEY LOOK

Unlike other big cats, male and female lions look quite different from each other. Many male lions have thick manes. They also have tufts of hair on their elbows, chest, and shoulders. Female lions—lionesses—do not have a mane or this extra hair trim.

Lions are well **camouflaged** on the African plains because of their tawny (yellowish-brown) fur. That color matches the color of grass and dry earth, making lions difficult to see. A few white lions have been known to exist, too.

Male lions average 350 to 400 pounds, and they measure just under nine feet in total length. Females weigh about 300 pounds. They average about eight feet in length.

African Lioness (Left) and Lion

WHERE THEY LIVE

Lions used to live in more places than almost any other mammal. Today they are limited to several African countries south of the Sahara Desert and to the Gir Forest of northwest India. Lions vanished from Europe about 2,000 years ago, and they are nearly gone from Asia.

Grassy plains are the lion's favorite living place, its **habitat**. It also likes "open" woodlands where trees are not too plentiful.

Lions sometimes travel through very dry country. In Africa, they have even wandered high up into the mountains.

Most lions live in the African nations of Kenya, Tanzania, Uganda, Zambia, Botswana, Southwest Africa, South Africa, and Angola.

African Lioness

Pride of Lions

HOW THEY LIVE

After hunts and big meals, lions like to rest and doze. A lion may spend over 20 hours each day resting.

Unlike many other cats, lions enjoy each other's company. They often live together in groups called **prides**. Members of the pride hunt together. The males defend the pride's **territory**, or living area, against other lions.

Lions normally move slowly—when they move at all. Still, they can swim, climb trees, jump nearly 12 feet in a bound, and run 35 miles per hour.

African Lioness

THE LION'S CUBS

A lioness looks for a mate when she is three to four years old. She can mate at any time of the year.

She carries her cubs, usually two to four, for three and one-half months before giving birth. The spotted cubs are blind for about a week after birth. The lioness keeps them hidden because baby lions have many enemies. If they are left alone, they may be killed by wild dogs, leopards, or even other lions.

Lions depend on their mother and the pride for food until they are a year and a half old.

Many lions die as babies, but lions can live up to 25 years in captivity.

African Lion Cub

PREDATOR AND PREY

Lions often hunt during the day. The lioness does most of the killing.

Lions have very keen senses, but they usually locate **prey**, the hunted animal, by sight. Moving very slowly and quietly, a lion **stalks** its prey. Then in the last few yards, it charges. The lion kills with its teeth and claws. It may eat 80 pounds of meat in one feeding!

A lion is the strongest **predator**, or hunting animal, in its habitat. Cheetahs and leopards stand aside. Still, lions can be hurt—even killed—by the hooves, horns, and feet of their prey.

Lions kill antelope, zebra, ostriches, and many other animals. They also **scavenge**, or eat animals which they themselves haven't killed.

African Lion with Wildebeest

LIONS AND PEOPLE

Lions have been a symbol of power and bravery for centuries. A former king of England was known as Richard The Lion-Hearted.

Lions have been objects of respect, and they have been objects of fear. But they have always been objects of human interest.

The ancient Egyptians, thousands of years ago, kept captive lions. The Romans, nearly two thousand years ago, pitted humans against lions in their bloody arena "games". In more recent years, lions have been major attractions in zoos and circuses.

Wild lions prefer to avoid people or at least ignore them. Over the years only a few lions have become man-eaters. Such lions are usually injured or too old to kill wild animals.

African Lioness

THE LION'S FUTURE

Lions have never been able to compete with people for land, and lion habitat is disappearing. Lions in India are carefully protected, but they number only about 200. In Africa, the growing human population is changing grassy plains—lion country—into farmland.

Although Africa is the lion's last stronghold, the big cats have been disappearing. The African lion population has slipped from perhaps 200,000 in 1950 to possibly as few as 50,000. As African crops and livestock herds increase, the number of lions will continue to decrease.

African wildlife parks protect many lions, especially in east Africa. Beyond the parks, however, the future of wild lions is not very bright.

Glossary

camouflage (KEM o flahj)—to hide by matching an animal's color to its surroundings

carnivore (KAR ni vore)—an animal that lives mostly or completely on meat

feline (FEE line)—any of the cats

habitat (HAB a tat)—the area in which an animal lives

predator (PRED a tor)—an animal that kills another animal for food

prey (PRAY)—an animal that is hunted for food by another animal

pride (PRIDE)—a group of lions with family ties

scavenge (SKA venge)—to feed on the remains of animals not killed by the feeder

species (SPEE sheez)—within a group of closely related animals, one certain kind

stalk (STAWK)—to hunt by slowly and quietly moving toward the victim

territory (TER rih tory)—a home area defended by certain animals that live within it

INDEX